SONGS AND DANCES OF IRELAND

Arranged for
RECORDER, FLUTE & PENNY V
Selected and arranged by Peter J. L

D0127417

WISE PUBLICATIONS
London/New York/Sydney/Cologne

Exclusive Distributors:
MUSIC SALES LIMITED
8/9 Frith Street, London W1V 5TZ
MUSIC SALES CORPORATION
24 East 22nd Street, New York, N.Y. 10010, U.S.A.
MUSIC SALES PTY. LIMITED
27 Clarendon Street, Artarmon, Sydney, NSW 2064, Australia

This book © Copyright 1982 by
Wise Publications
ISBN 0 7119 0099 X
Order No. AM 31402

Designed by Howard Brown
Cover illustration by Tony Meeuwissen

Music Sales complete catalogue lists thousands of titles
and is free from your local music book shop, or direct from
Music Sales Limited. Please send 50p in stamps for postage
to Music Sales Limited, 8/9 Frith Street, London W1V 5TZ.

Printed and bound in Great Briain by
Anchor Brendon Ltd, Tiptree, Essex

Contents

DEAR OLD DONEGAL

Words & Music Steve Graham

(1) It seems like on - ly yes - ter-day I sailed from out of
(2) give a par-ty when I go home they'll come from near and

Cork, _____ A wan - der - er from Er - in's Isle I
far, _____ They'll line the roads for miles and miles with

land - ed in New York. _____ There was-n't a soul _ to
I - rish jaunt - in' cars. _____ The spi - rits-'ll flow _ and

greet me there, a stran - ger on your shore, _____ But
we'll be gay, we'll fill your hearts with joy, _____ The

I - rish luck was with me here and rich - es came ga-
pi - per'll play an I - rish reel to greet the Yan - kee

-lore. _____ And now that I'm go - in' back a - gain to
boy. _____ We'll dance _ and sing the whole night long, such

dear old Er - in's Isle, _____ My friends will meet me
fun as nev - er seen, _____ The lads'll be decked in

THE GARDEN WHERE THE PRATIES GROW

Words & Music by Johnny Patterson

3. Says I, "My pretty Kathleen, I'm tired of single life,
And if you've no objection, sure, I'll make you my sweet wife."
She answered me right modestly and curtsied very low,
"Oh, you're welcome to the garden where the praties grow."

4. Says I, "My pretty Kathleen, I hope that you'll agree,"
She was not like your city girls who say you're making free;
Says she, "I'll ax my parents, and tomorrow I'll let you know,
If you'll meet me in the garden where the praties grow."

5. Oh, the parents they consented and we're bless'd with children three,
Two boys just like their mother and a girl the image of me,
And now we're goin' to train them up the way they ought to go,
For to dig in the garden where the praties grow.

6. (as 2nd)

SLATTERY'S MOUNTED FUT

Traditional

(1) You've heard of Jul - ius
(2) Well, first we rec - on-
(3) "We'll cross the ditch," our
(4) They reach'd the moun - tain

Cæ - sar, and of great Na - po - leon too, _____ And
-noi - tred round O' - Sul - li - van's She - been, _____ It
lead - er cried "and take the foe in flank," _____ But
safe - ly, though all stiff and sore with cramp; _____ Each

how the Cork Mil - i - tia beat the Turks at Wat - er-
used to be the "Shop House," but we called it "The Can-
yells of con - stern - a - tion here a - rose from ev - 'ry
took a wet of whisk - y nate to dis - si - pate the

-loo; But there's a page of glo - ry that, as
-teen;" But there we saw a no - tice which the
rank, For post - ed high up - on a tree we
damp, And when they load - ed all their pipes, bowld

yet, re-mains un-cut, And that's the war-like
brav-est heart un-nerved, "All li-quor must be
ve-ry plain-ly saw, "Tres-pass-ers pros-e-
Slat-ter-y ups and said, "To-day's im-mor-tal

sto-ry of the Slat-ter-y Mount-ed Fut. This
set-tled for be-fore the drink is served." So
-cut-ed, in ac-cord-ance with the law." "We're
fight will be re-mem-bered by the dead: I

gal-lant corps was or-gan-ised by Slat-ter-y's eld-est
on we marched, but soon a-gain each war-ri-or's heart grew
foiled," ex-claimed bold Slat-ter-y, "here ends our grand cam-
nev-er shall for-get," says he, "while this brave heart shall

son. A no-ble mind-ed poach-er with a
pale, For ris-ing high in front of us we
-paign, 'Tis mere-ly throw-ing life a-way to
beat, The eag-er way ye fol-lowed when I

dou-ble-breast-ed gun. And man-y a head was
saw the Coun-ty Jail; And when the arm-y
face that mear-in' dhrain, I'm not as bowld as
head-e the re-treat. Ye pre-ferred the sold-

o-pen'd aye, and man-y an eye was shut, While
faced a-bout, 'twas just in time to find A
li-ons, but I'm brav-er than a hen, And
ier's max-im, when de-sist-ing from the strife, 'Best be a

8

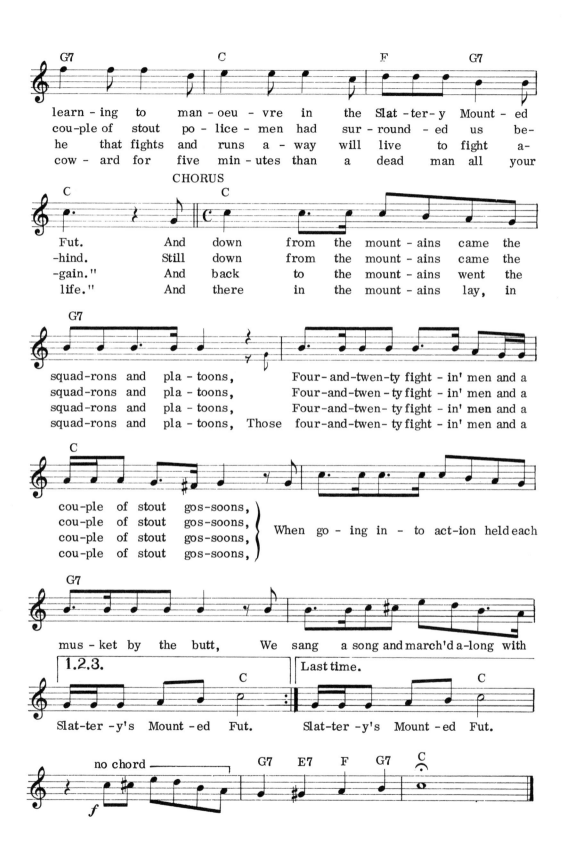

learn - ing to man - oeu - vre in the Slat -ter- y Mount - ed
cou -ple of stout po - lice - men had sur - round - ed us be-
he that fights and runs a - way will live to fight a-
cow - ard for five min - utes than a dead man all your

CHORUS

Fut. And down from the mount - ains came the
-hind. Still down from the mount - ains came the
-gain." And back to the mount - ains went the
life." And there in the mount - ains lay, in

squad-rons and pla - toons, Four- and-twen-ty fight - in' men and a
squad-rons and pla - toons, Four-and-twen - ty fight - in' men and a
squad-rons and pla - toons, Four-and-twen- ty fight - in' men and a
squad-rons and pla - toons, Those four-and-twen- ty fight - in' men and a

cou -ple of stout gos-soons, ⎫
cou -ple of stout gos-soons, ⎬ When go - ing in - to act-ion held each
cou -ple of stout gos-soons, ⎭
cou -ple of stout gos-soons,

mus - ket by the butt, We sang a song and march'd a-long with

1.2.3.

Slat-ter -y's Mount - ed Fut.

Last time.

Slat-ter -y's Mount -ed Fut.

no chord ⌐————⌐ G7 E7 F G7 C

f

9

WHISTLING GYPSY/GYPSY ROVER

Words & Music by Leo Maguire

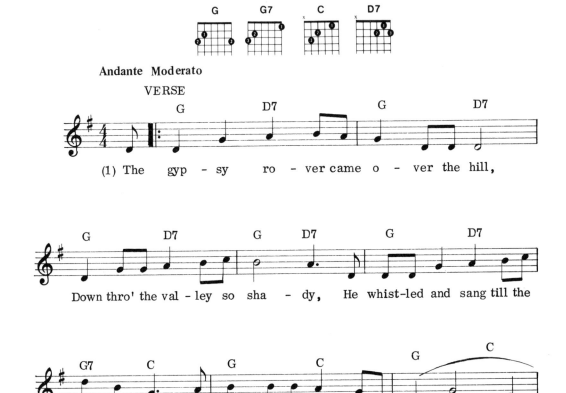

Andante Moderato

VERSE

(1) The gyp - sy ro - ver came o - ver the hill,

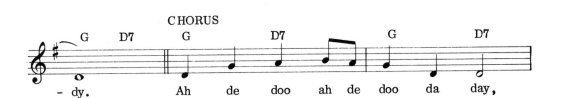

Down thro' the val - ley so sha - dy, He whist-led and sang till the green-woods rang, And he won the heart of a la - - dy.

CHORUS

Ah de doo ah de doo da day, Ah de doo ah de day de, He whist-led and sang till the

green - woods rang, And he won the heart of a

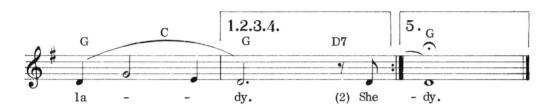

la - - dy. (2) She - dy.

(2) She left her father's castle gate,
She left her fair young lover,
She left her servants and her state,
To follow the gypsy rover.

(3) Her father saddled up his fastest steed,
He ranged the valleys over,
He sought his daughter at great speed,
And the whistling gypsy rover.

(4) He came at last to a mansion fine,
Down by the river Clady,
And there was music and there was wine,
For the gypsy and his lady.

(5) "He is no gypsy, father dear,
But lord of these lands all over,
I'm going to stay 'til my dying day,
With my whistling gypsy rover."

LONDONDERRY AIR (ACUSHLA MINE)

Traditional

Plaintively

(1) A - cush - la, mine, the sing - ing birds are
mine, your lips are ev - er
mine, when birds a - gain are

call - ing, The call of love, that's meant for lov - ers
smil - ing, They smiled their way in - to my long - ing
sing - ing, Their ma - ting song, and all the land is

true, 'Tis Au - tumn time, and where the leaves are
heart, Your ro - guish eyes to me are so be-
gay, When, at the church, the wed - ding bells are

fall - ing, A - lone — I — wait, to beg a word with
-guil - ing, I pray — the — Saints, that nev - er we may
ring - ing, Ma - vour - neen, — dear, 'twill be a hap - py

| | F | B♭ | F | | C7 | | F | | B♭ | | F |

you.   'Tis   of   my   love,   my   love   I   would   be
part.   When   Win- ter   comes,   and   all   the   world   is
day.   And through the   years   no   mat - ter   what   the

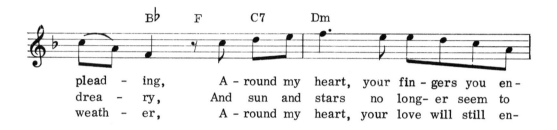

| | B♭ | F | | C7 | | Dm |

plead   -   ing,   A - round my   heart,   your fin - gers you   en-
drea   -   ry,   And   sun   and   stars   no   long- er   seem   to
weath   -   er,   A - round my   heart,   your love   will   still   en-

| G7 | | C7 | | | F7 | | B♭ |

-twine,   The   birds   a - bove,   they   know   how   much   I'm
shine,   The   world   is   dark,   and   I   am   sad   and
-twine,   We'll   wan - der   on,   as   long   as   we're   to-

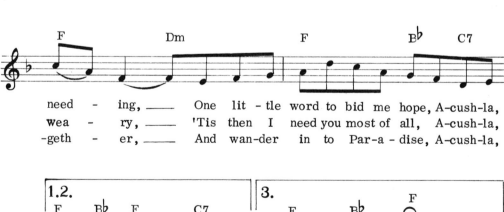

| F | | Dm | | F | | B♭ | C7 |

need   -   ing, _____   One   lit - tle word to bid me hope, A-cush-la,
wea   -   ry, _____   'Tis   then   I   need you most of all, A-cush-la,
-geth   -   er, _____   And   wan-der   in   to   Par-a-dise, A-cush-la,

1.2.

| F | B♭ | F | | C7 |

3.

| F | | B♭ | | F |

mine.   (2)   A - cush - la,   mine. _____
        (3)   A - cush - la,

FINNEGAN'S WAKE

Traditional

(1) Tim Fin-ne-gan lived in Wal - kin Street, a

gen-tle-man I - rish might -y odd, He had a tongue both

rich and sweet, and to rise in the world, he car-ried a hod. Now

Tim had a sort of a tip - pling way, with a love of the li-quor poor

Tim was born, and to help him in his way each day, he'd a

drop of the cra - tur ev' - ry morn!

CHORUS

Whack fol de da now dance to your part - ner,

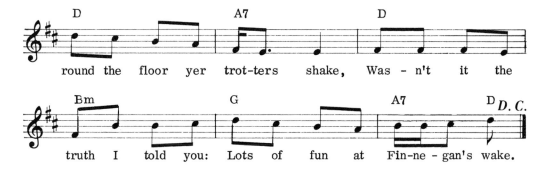

round the floor yer trot-ters shake, Was-n't it the

truth I told you: Lots of fun at Fin-ne-gan's wake.

D. C.

(2) One morning Tim was rather full,
    His head felt heavy which made him shake,
    He fell from the ladder and broke his skull,
    So they carried him home, his corpse to wake.
    They wrapped him up in a nice clean sheet,
    And layed him out upon the bed,
    With a gallon of whiskey at his feet,
    And a barrel of porter at his head.
    CHORUS

(3) His friends assembled at the wake,
    And Mrs. Finnegan called for lunch.
    First they brought in tay and cakes,
    Then pipes, tobacco and whiskey punch.
    Miss Biddy O'Brien began to cry,
    "Such a neat clean corpse did you ever see?"
    "Yerrah, Tim avourneen, why did you die?"
    "Ah, hold yer tongue" says Paddy Magee.
    CHORUS

(4) Then Biddy O'Connor took up the moan,
    "Oh Biddy," says she, "You're wrong, I'm sure."
    But Biddy gave her a belt in the gob,
    And left her sprawling on the floor.
    Of then the might war did rage,
    'Twas woman to woman and man to man,
    Shillelagh law did all engage,
    And a row and ruction soon began.
    CHORUS

(5) Then Micky Maloney ducked his head,
    When a noggin of whiskey flew at him,
    It missed him, falling on the bed,
    The liquor splattered over Tim.
    Bedad he revives and see how he rises,
    And Timothy rising from the bed,
    Says "Fling your whiskey round like blazes,
    Thunderin' Jaysus, did you think me dead?"
    CHORUS

FORTY SHADES OF GREEN

Words & Music by Johnny Cash

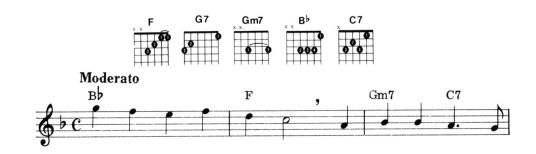

Moderato

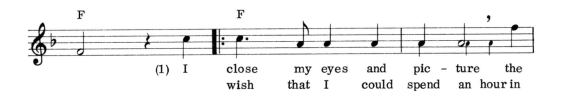

(1) I close my eyes and pic - ture the
wish that I could spend an hour in

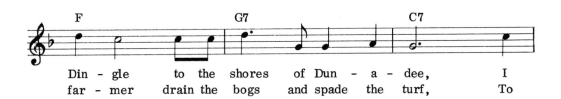

em - 'rald of the sea, From the fish - ing boats at
Dub - lin's churn-ing surf. I would love to watch the

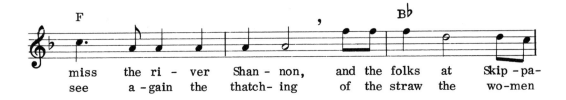

Din - gle to the shores of Dun - a - dee, I
far - mer drain the bogs and spade the turf, To

F

miss the ri - ver Shan - non, and the folks at Skip - pa -
see a - gain the thatch- ing of the straw the wo - men

-ree. The Moor-lands and the Mid-lands with them
glean. I'd walk from Cork to Liam to see the

for-ty shades of green.
for-ty shades of green. But most of all I

miss a girl in Tip-pe-ra-ry town. And

most of all I miss her lips, as soft as ei-der-

-down. A-gain I want to see and do the

things we've done and seen, Where the breeze is sweet as

Shal-i-mar and there's for-ty shades of green (2) I green

PATSY FAGAN
(THE DACENT IRISH BOY)
Words & Music by Thomas P. Keenan

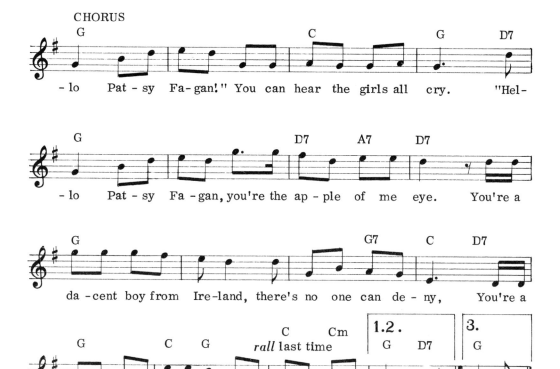

CHORUS

-lo Pat-sy Fa-gan!" You can hear the girls all cry. "Hel-
-lo Pat-sy Fa-gan, you're the ap-ple of me eye. You're a
da-cent boy from Ire-land, there's no one can de-ny, You're a
ra-rem ta-rem div-il may ca-rem da-cent I-rish boy." (2) Now boy.___

(2) Now if there's one among you,
    Would like to marry me,
    I'll take her to a little home
    Across the Irish Sea.
    I'll dress her up in Satin,
    And please her all I can,
    And let her people see that I'm
    A dacent Irish boy.
    CHORUS

(3) The day that I left Ireland,
    'Twas many years ago.
    I left me home in Antrim
    Where the pigs and praties grow.
    But since I left auld Ireland,
    It's always been my plan,
    To let the people see that I'm
    A dacent Irishman,
    CHORUS

LET HIM GO LET HIM TARRY

Traditional

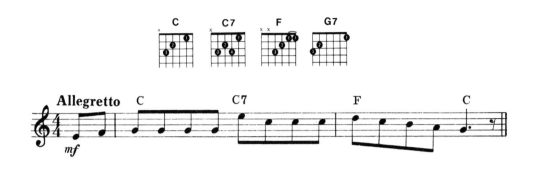

(1)   Fare-well to cold winter,
(2) He   wrote —— me a let-ter say-ing
(3)   Some — of his friends — had a
(4) He can go   to his old mother now, and

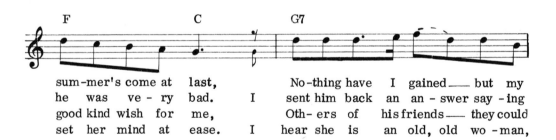

sum-mer's come at   last,   No-thing have   I gained —— but my
he was ve - ry   bad.   I   sent him back an an - swer say - ing
good kind wish for   me,   Oth- ers of   his friends —— they could
set her mind at   ease.   I   hear she is an old, old wo -man,

true love I have lost. I'll sing and I'll be hap - py like the
I was aw - ful glad. He wrote to me an - oth - er say - ing
hang me on a tree, But soon I'll let them see my love, and
ve - ry hard to please. It's slight - ing me and talk - ing ill is

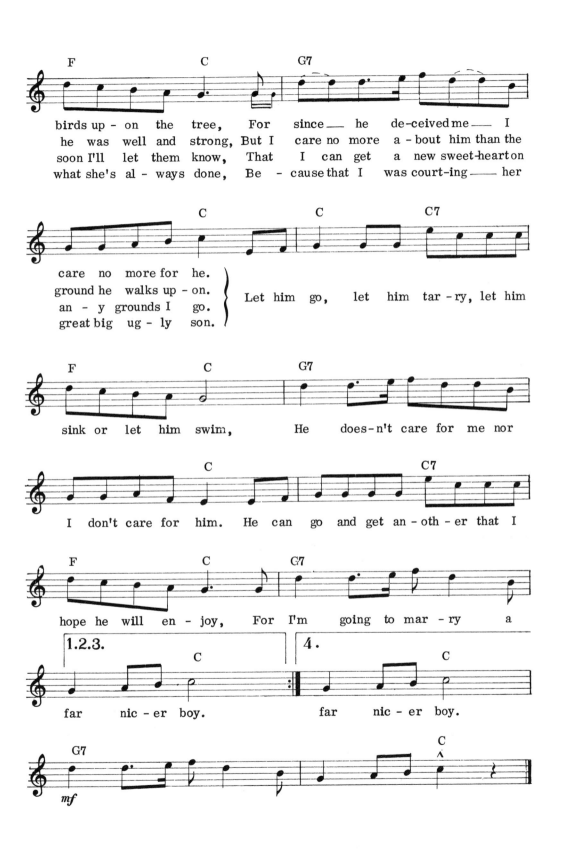

birds up - on the tree, For since ___ he de-ceived me ___ I
he was well and strong, But I care no more a - bout him than the
soon I'll let them know, That I can get a new sweet-heart on
what she's al - ways done, Be - cause that I was court-ing ___ her

care no more for he.
ground he walks up - on.
an - y grounds I go.
great big ug - ly son.

} Let him go, let him tar - ry, let him

sink or let him swim, He does-n't care for me nor

I don't care for him. He can go and get an - oth - er that I

hope he will en - joy, For I'm going to mar - ry a

1.2.3.

far nic - er boy.

4.

far nic - er boy.

mf

THE BLACK VELVET BAND

Traditional

(1) 'Twas in the town of Tra - lee, ap-
-pren-tice to trade I was bound, With a - plen-ty of bright a-
- muse-ment to see the days of my youth go a-
-round. Mis - for-tune and trou-ble came o'er me, which
caused me to stray from the land, Far a -way from my friends and re-
- la - tions, to fol - low the Black Vel - vet Band.

CHORUS

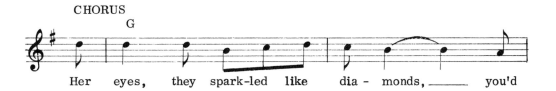

Her eyes, they spark-led like dia - monds, _____ you'd

think she was queen o' the land, _____ With her hair thrown o-ver her

shoul - ders, tied up with a Black Vel-vet Band. _____

(2) As I went walking down broadway, not intending to stay very long,
I met with a frolicksome damsel as she came a tripping along.
A watch she pulled out of her pocket and slipped it right into my hand,
On the very first day that I met her: bad luck to the Black Velvet Band.
CHORUS

(3) Before the judge and the jury the both of us had to appear,
And a gentleman swore to the jewellery - the case against us was clear.
For seven years transportation right unto Van Dieman's Land,
Far away from my friends and relations to follow her Black Velvet Band.
CHORUS

(3) Oh, all you brave young Irish lads, a warning take by me,
Beware of the pretty young damsels that are roamin' in Tralee.
They'll treat you to whiskey and porter until you're unable to stand,
And before you have time for to leave them, you are unto Van Dieman's Land.
CHORUS

THE SPINNING WHEEL

Traditional

Andante con moto

(1) Mel - low the moon-light to shine is be - gin - ning,

Close by the win - dow young Eil - een is spin - ning,

Bent o'er the fire her blind grand-mo - ther, sit - ting, Is

croon - ing and moan - ing and drow - si - ly knit - ting.

CHORUS

Mer - ri - ly, cheer - i - ly, nois - i - ly whirr - ing,

Swings the wheel, spins the wheel, while the foot's stirr - ing,

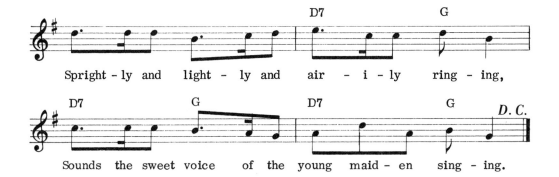

Sprightly and lightly and airily ringing,
Sounds the sweet voice of the young maiden singing.

(2) "Eileen, a chara,* I hear someone tapping,"
"'Tis the ivy, dear mother, against the glass flapping,"
"Eily, I surely hear somebody sighing,"
"'Tis the sound, mother dear, of the autumn winds dying."
CHORUS

(3) "What's that noise that I hear at the window I wonder?
"'Tis the liitle birds chirping at the holly-bush under,"
"What makes you be pushing and moving your stool on?"
"And singing all wrong that old song of Coolin?"
CHORUS

(4) There's a form at the casement, the form of her true love,
And he whispers with face bent, "Im waiting for you, love"
"Get up on the stool, through the lattice step lightly,
And we'll rove in the grove while the moon's shining brightly."
CHORUS

(5) The maid shakes her head, on her lips lays her fingers,
Steals up from the seat, longs to go and yet lingers;
A frightened glance turns to her drowsy grandmother,
Puts one foot on the stool, spins the wheel with the other.
CHORUS

(6) Lazily, easily, swings now the wheel round,
Slowly and lowly is heard now the reel's sound;
Noiseless and light to the lattice above her
The maid steps, then leaps to the arms of her lover.

Last Chorus:
Slower, and slower, and slower the wheel swings,
Lower, and lower, and lower the reel rings;
Ere the reel and the wheel stopped their spinning and moving,
Through the grove the young lovers by moonlight are roving.

*Pronounced "Kaura"

KILLARNEY

Traditional

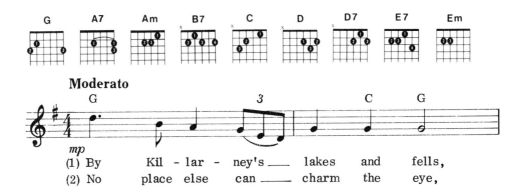

Moderato

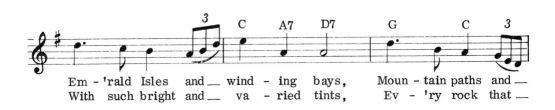

(1) By Kil - lar - ney's ___ lakes and fells,
(2) No place else can ___ charm the eye,

Em - 'rald Isles and ___ wind - ing bays, Moun - tain paths and ___
With such bright and ___ va - ried tints, Ev - 'ry rock that ___

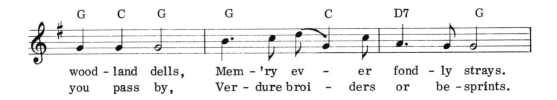

wood - land dells, Mem - 'ry ev - er fond - ly strays.
you pass by, Ver - dure broi - ders or be - sprints.

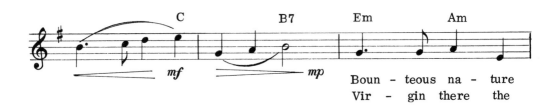

Boun - teous na - ture
Vir - gin there the

loves all lands,— Beau - ty wan - ders— ev - 'ry - where,
green grass grows,— Ev - 'ry morn— Spring's—na - tal — day;

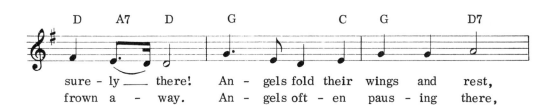

Foot - prints leaves on ma - ny strands,— But her home is —
Bright hued ber - ries daff the snows,— Smil - ing Win-ter's —

sure - ly — there! An - gels fold their wings and rest,
frown a - way. An - gels oft - en paus - ing there,

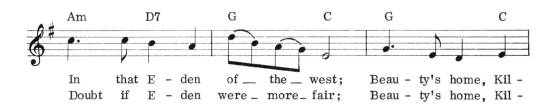

In that E - den of — the — west; Beau - ty's home, Kil -
Doubt if E - den were — more— fair; Beau - ty's home, Kil -

- lar - ney, Heav'ns re - flex,— Kil - lar - ney.
- lar - ney, Heav'ns re - flex,— Kil - lar - ney.

I'll Take You Home Again Kathleen

Traditional

And tears be-dim your lov-ing eyes.

CHORUS
mf Oh! I will take you back, Kath-leen,

To where your heart will feel no pain,

And when the fields are fresh and green,

I'll take you to your home a-gain!

(2) I know you love me, Kathleen dear,
Your heart was ever fond and true,
I always feel when you are near
That life holds nothing dear but you.
The smiles that once you gave to me,
I scarcely ever see them now,
Though many, many times I see
A dark'ning shadow on your brow.
CHORUS

(3) To that dear home across the sea
My Kathleen shall again return,
And when thy old friends welcome thee,
Thy loving heart will cease to yearn.
Where laughs the little silver stream,
Beside your mother's humble cot,
And brightest rays of sunshine gleam,
There all your grief will be forgot.
CHORUS

O'RAFFERTY'S MOTOR CAR

Words & Music by Tommie Connor

(1) Now Din-ny O'Raf-fer-ty's mo-tor car is the great-est I de-clare, __ It's made up of bits and piec-es that he's picked up here and there, __ The en-gine must be ag-es old but it's still got lots of power, __ With a gal-lon of stout in the pet-rol tank it does

(2) two of the wheels are tri-ang-u-lar and the third one's off a pram. __ The forth is the last re-main-ing wheel from off a Dub-lin tram, __ The num-ber plate's in Gae-lic and the plugs won't ev-en spark, __ And the chas-sis came off of a tink-er's cart that col-

(3) go for a ride in that mo-tor car and you'll end up with the shakes. __ The road from Cork to Dub-lin is a vale of pains and aches, __ When traf-fic lights turn red a-head then you best jump out the door, __ For the mo-ment that Din-ny treads on the brake, then his

CHORUS

nine - ty miles an hour. ___)
-lapsed in Phoe- nix Park. ___ } Oh what a won-der-ful mo-tor car, It's the
foot goes thro' the floor. ___)

great - est ev - er seen. ____ It used to be black as me

Fath - er's hat, now it's for - ty shades of green. ____ On

tee vee and the ra - di - o and in ev - 'ry pub - lic

bar, ____ The burn - ing quest - ion of the day is O' -

Raf - fer-ty's mo - tor car. ____ (2) Now car. ___
(3) Now
(4) Now
(5) Now

(4) Now if you could see the upholstery, then your eyes would start to pop,
It's nothing but empty beer crates with a load of sacks on top.
The windscreen's gone to Lord knows where and there's moth balls in the horn,
And I reckon he'd only get half a quid if he took it to the pawn.
(CHORUS)

(5) Now Dinny was driving around last week when the engine did the splits,
It went up in smoke and nearly blew O'Connell Street to bits!
They search'd for Dinny and found that he'd landed up by heck,
Away on top of the G.P.O. with his L-plates round his neck.
(CHORUS)

COCKLES AND MUSSELS

Traditional

o! ___ A - live, a - live - o! ___ Cry-ing

"Cock-les and mus-sels a - live, a - live - o!"

2. She was a fishmonger, but sure 'twas no wonder,
   For so were her father and mother before,
   And they each wheel'd their barrow,
   Through streets broad and narrow,
   Crying "Cockles and mussels alive, alive-o!"
   CHORUS

3. She died of a fever, and no one could save her,
   And that was the end of sweet Molly Malone,
   But her ghost wheels her barrow,
   Through streets broad and narrow,
   Crying "Cockles and mussels alive, alive-o!"
   CHORUS

The Wearin' O' The Green

Traditional

Tan - dy and he took me by the hand, Said

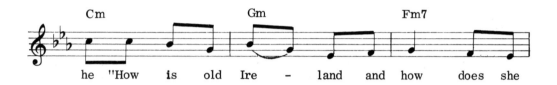

he "How is old Ire - land and how does she

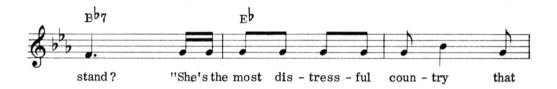

stand? "She's the most dis - tress - ful coun - try that

ev - er could be seen, For they're hang - ing men and

wo - men for the wear - ing of the green."

(2) Then since the colour we must wear is England's cruel red,
No Irishman must now forget the blood that has been shed.
They may take the shamrock from our breasts and cast it on the sod,
But it will take root where'er it rests though underfoot it's trod.
When the law can stop the blades of grass from growing as they grow,
And when the leaves in summertime their colours daren't show,
Then I'll take down the shamrock that I wear on Paddy's e'en,
But until that day I'll live and die still wearin' o' the green.

MICK MCGUIRE

Traditional

(1) Oh, me name is Mick Mc - Guire, ___ and I'll
(2) Now, the first time that I met her was at the

quick - ly tell to you, Of a young girl I ad-
dance at Tar - ma - gee, And I ver - y kind - ly

- mired ___ called ___ Ka - ty Don - a - hue. She was
asked her if she's dance a step with me. Then I

fair and fat and for - ty, and be - lieve me when I
asked if I could see her home, if I'd be go-ing her

say, That when - ev - er I came in at the door you could
way, And when - ev - er I'd come in at the door you could

hear her mam - my say: }
hear her mam - my say: }

"John- ny, get up from the

fire; get up and give the man a sate. Can't you

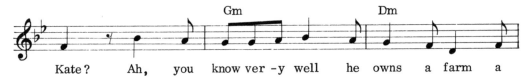

see it's Mis-ter Mc - Guire,___ and he's court-ing your sis - ter

Kate? Ah, you know ver -y well he owns a farm a

wee bit out of the town. Ar-ragh, get up out of that, you

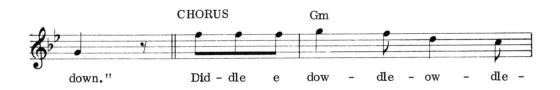

im - pu - dent brat, and let Mis - ter Mc - Guire sit

CHORUS

down." Did - dle e dow - dle - ow - dle -

- ow - dle, did-dle e dow - dle -ow - dle -ow, Did-dle e

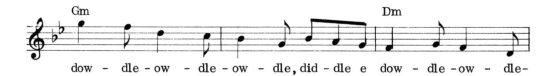

dow - dle - ow - dle - ow - dle, did - dle e dow - dle - ow - dle-

- ow. "Ah, you know ve - ry well he owns that farm a

wee bit out of the town. Ar-ragh, get up out of that, you

im - pu-dent brat, and let Mis-ter Mc - Guire sit down."

(3) Ah, but now that we are married, shure, her mother's changed her mind,
Just because I spent the legacy her father left behind.
She hasn't got the decency to bid me time of day;
Now whenever I come in at the door you'd hear the auld one say:
"Johnny, come up the fire, come up; you're sitting in a draft.
Can't you see it's auld McGuire, and he nearly drives me daft?
Ah, I don't know what gets into him, for he's always on the tare.
Arragh, just sit where you are and never you dare,
To give auld McGuire the chair."

CHORUS
Diddle e dowdle-owdle-owdle,
Diddle e dowdle-oudle-ow,
Diddle e dowdle-owdle-owdle,
Diddle e dowdle owdle-ow.
"Ah, I don't know what gets into him,
For he's always on the tare.
Arragh, just sit where you are and never you dare,
To give auld McGuire the chair."

THE LAST ROSE OF SUMMER

Traditional

Slowly

(1) 'Tis the last rose of ____ sum - mer, left ____
(2) I'll not leave thee, thou ____ lone one, to ____

bloom - ing ____ a - lone, ____ All her love - ly com -
pine on ____ the ____ stem, ____ Since the love - ly are

-pan - ions are ____ fad - ed ____ and ____ gone; ____ No ____
sleep-ing, go ____ sleep thou ____ with ____ them. ____ Thus ____

flow'r of ____ her ____ kin - dred, no ____ rose - bud ____ is ____
kind - ly ____ I ____ scat - ter thy ____ leaves o'er ____ the ____

nigh, ____ ____ To re - flect back ____ her ____
bed, ____ ____ Where thy mates of ____ the ____

blush-es, or ____ give ____ sigh ____ for ____ sigh. ____
gar - den lie ____ scent - less and ____ dead. ____

D.C. al Fine

MASTER MCGRATH

Traditional

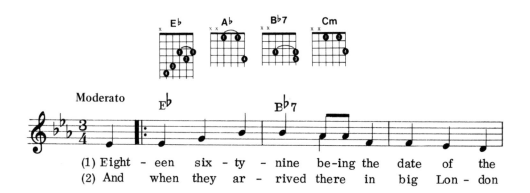

(1) Eight - een six - ty - nine be-ing the date of the
(2) And when they ar - rived there in big Lon - don

year, The Wa - ter - loo sports - men, they
town, The great Eng - lish sports - men, they

all did ap - pear, To win the great
all gath - ered 'round, One of the

prize and to bear it a - way, Nev - er
gen - tle - men gave a ha - ha, "Is

D.C. al Fine

count - ing on Ire - land and Mas - ter Mc - Grath.
that the great dog you call Mas - ter Mc - Grath?"

3. Lord Lurgon stepped forward and he said, "Gentlemen,
   If there are any among you have money to spend,
   For your great English greyhound I don't care a straw,
   Five thousand to one upon Master McGrath."

4. White Rose stood uncovered, the great English pride;
   Her trainer and owner were both by her side.
   They led her away and the crowd cried, "Hurrah!"
   For the pride of all England and Master McGrath.

5. As Rose and the Master, they both ran along,
   "I wonder," said Rose, "what took you from your home.
   You should have stayed there in your Irish domain,
   And not come to gain laurels on Albion's plains."

6. "I know," said McGrath, "we have wild heather bogs,
   But you'll find in old Ireland we have good men and dogs.
   Lead on, bold Britannia, give none of your jaw;
   Snuff that up your nostrils," said Master McGrath.

7. The hare she led on, what a beautiful view,
   As swift as the wind o'er the green fields she flew.
   He jumped on her back and he held up his paw;
   "Three cheers for old Ireland," said Master McGrath.

8. I've known many greyhounds that filled me with pride,
   In the days that are gone and it can't be denied,
   But the greatest and the bravest the world ever saw,
   Was our champion of champions, brave Master McGrath.

EILEEN ALANNAH

Traditional

© Copyright 1982 Dorsey Brothers Music Ltd, London
All rights reserved. International copyright secured.

- vour - neen thy dear face I see ___ at the door,
heart is now bleed-ing to it's in - ner - most core,

Ei - leen A - lan - nah, Au - gus As - thore.
Ei - leen A - lan - nah, Au - gus As - thore.

CHORUS

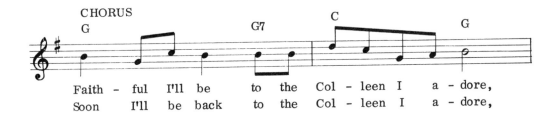

Faith - ful I'll be to the Col - leen I a - dore,
Soon I'll be back to the Col - leen I a - dore,

Ei - leen A - lan - nah, Au - gus As-thore,
Ei - leen A - lan - nah, Au - gus As-thore,

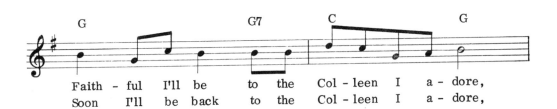

Faith - ful I'll be to the Col - leen I a - dore,
Soon I'll be back to the Col - leen I a - dore,

Ei - leen A - lan - nah, Au - gus As-thore.
Ei - leen A - lan - nah, Au - gus As-thore.

WITH MY SHILLELAGH UNDER MY ARM

Words & Music by Raymond Wallace and Billy O'Brien

(1) Shure, I'm tired of roam-in' round and so I'm gon-na pack my grip, And I'm off to book my pas-sage on a might-y pow'r-ful ship. I'll be bound to send a tel-e-gram the day I reach the quay, Just to tell them in a week or two they'll be ex-pect-in' me.

(2) Shure, I'm feel-in' might-y fine and I've got bags o' mon-ey too, And I mean to give the folks at home a pro-per I-rish do. There'll be such a wel-come wait-in' for your hum-ble on the mat, I can just i-ma-gine peo-ple say-in' "Och how are ye, Pat?"

CHORUS

With my shil-le-lagh un-der my arm, And a twin-kle in my eye, I'll be

off to Tip-per-ar-y in the morn - in', With my shil-

-le - lagh un-der my arm, And a "Too-la-roo-la-li," I'll be

wel-come in the home that I was born in._____ My

Moth-er's told the neigh-bours that I'm gon-na set-tle down,____

Phil the Flu-ter's com-in' out to play me round the town, With my shil-

-le - lagh un-der my arm, And a twin-kle in my eye, I'll be

off to Tip-per-ar-y in the morn - in'._____

-in'. _____ *mf*

45

BELIEVE ME IF ALL THOSE ENDEARING YOUNG CHARMS

Traditional

love - li - ness fade as it will; ____

____ And a - round the dear ru - in each

wish of my heart, Would en - twine it - self

ver - dant - ly still. ____

2. It is not while beauty and youth are thine own,
   And thy cheeks unprofaned by a tear,
   That the fervour and faith of a soul can be known,
   To which time will but make thee more dear.
   No, the heart that has truly loved, never forgets,
   But as truly loves on to the close;
   As the sunflower turns on her god, when he sets,
   The same look that she turned when he rose.

MacNamara's Band

Words John J. Stamford
Music Shamus O'Connor

Hen-nes-sy Ten-nes-sy too-tles the flute, my word! 'tis some-thing
grand, Oh! a cred - it to Ould Ire - land, boys, is
Mac - na - ma - ra's band! Tra-la - la la la, Tra-la-la
la la, Tra - la - la la la la la la la la
la, Tra -la -la la la, ____ Tra-la-la la la, Tra-la-
-la la la la la la la la la. (2) When la.
(3) We

2. Whenever an election's on, we play on either side,
   The way we play our fine ould airs fills Irish hearts with pride.
   Oh! If poor Tom Moore was living now, he'd make yez understand,
   That one could do him justice like ould Macnamara's band.
   (When the drums go bang etc.)

3. We play at wakes and weddings, and at ev'ry county ball,
   And at any great man's funeral we play the "Dead March in Saul";
   When the Prince of Wales to Ireland came, he shook me by the hand,
   And said he'd never heard the like of Macnamara's band.
   (When the drums go bang etc.)

THE MOUNTAINS OF MOURNE

Traditional

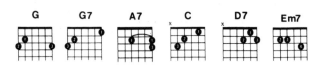

(1) Oh! Ma - ry! this Lon - don's a won - der - ful

sight, Wid the peo - ple here work - in' by day and by

night; They don't sow pot - a - tes, nor bar - ley, nor

wheat, But there's gangs o' them dig - gin' for gold in the

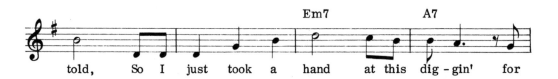

street; At least, when I axed them that's what I was

told, So I just took a hand at this dig - gin' for

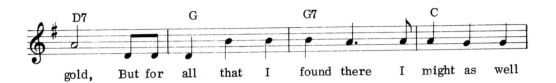

gold,   But for   all   that   I   found there   I   might as   well

be,   Where the Moun-tains o'   Mourne___ sweep down to   the   sea.

(2) I believe that, when writin', a wish you express'd,
As to how the fine ladies in London were dress'd.
Well if you'll believe me, when axed to a ball,
Faith, they don't wear a top to their dresses at all.
Oh, I've seen them meself, and you could not, in thraith,
Say if they were bound for a ball or a bath.
Don't be startin' them fashions now, Mary Macree,
Where the Mountains o' Mourne sweep down to the sea.

(3) I've seen England's King from the top of a bus,
I never knew him, tho' he means to know us;
And tho' by the Saxon we once were oppress'd,
Still I cheer'd (God forgive me) I cheer'd wid the rest.
And now that he's visited Erin's green shore,
We'll be much better friends than we've been heretofore,
When we've got all we want we're as quiet as can be,
Where the Mountains o' Mourne sweep down to the sea.

(4) You remember young Peter O'Loughlin, of course?
Well, now he is here at the head o' the force.
I met him today, I was crossin' the Strand,
And he stopp'd the whole street wid a wave of his hand.
And there we stood talkin' of days that are gone,
While the whole population of London look'd on.
But for all these great powers he's wishful, like me,
To be back where dark Mourne sweeps down to the sea.

(5) There's beautiful girls here, Oh! niver mind!
Wid beautiful shapes nature niver design'd,
And lovely complexions all roses and crame,
But O'Loughlin remark'd wid regard to the same,
That if at those roses you venture to sip,
The colours might all come away on your lip.
So I'll wait for the wild rose that's waitin' for me,
Where the Mountains o' Mourne sweep down to the sea.

ST PATRICK WAS A GENTLEMAN

Traditional

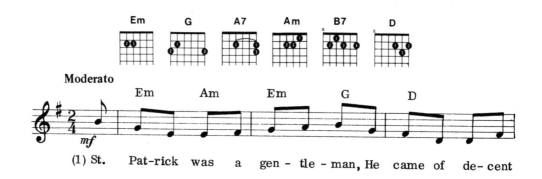

Moderato

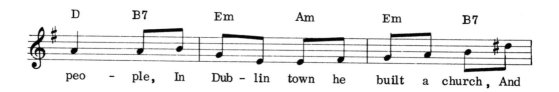

(1) St. Pat-rick was a gen - tle -man, He came of de - cent

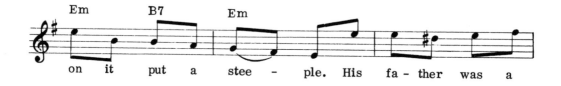

peo - ple, In Dub - lin town he built a church, And

on it put a stee - ple. His fa - ther was a

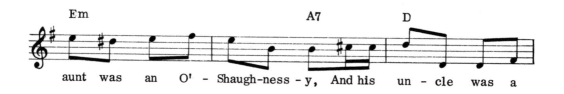

Call - a -ghan, His moth - er was a Bra - dy, His

aunt was an O' - Shaugh-ness -y, And his un - cle was a

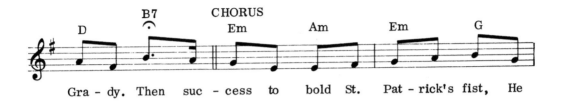

Gra - dy. Then suc - cess to bold St. Pat - rick's fist, He

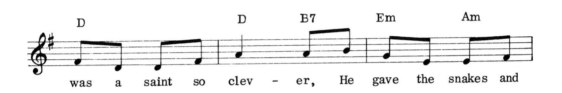

was a saint so clev - er, He gave the snakes and

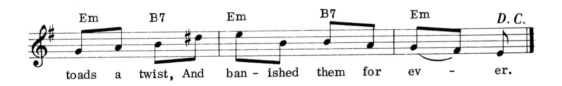

toads a twist, And ban - ished them for ev - er.

(2) There's not a mile in Ireland's Isle where the dirty vermin musters,
Where'er he put his dear forefoot he murder'd them in clusters.
The toads went hop, the frogs went plop, slap dash into the water,
And the beasts committed suicide to save themselves from slaughter.
CHORUS

(3) Nine hundred thousand vipers blue he charm'd with sweet discourses,
And dined on them at Killaloo in soups and second courses.
When blind worms crawling on the grass disgusted all the nation,
He gave them a rise and open'd their eyes to a sense of their situation.
CHORUS

(4) The Wicklow hills are very high, and so's the hill of Howth, sir,
But there's a hill much higher still, Ay, higher than them both, sir.
'Twas on the top of this high hill St. Patrick preach'd the "sarmint,"
He drove the frogs into the bogs, and bothered all the "varmint."
CHORUS

THE ROSE OF TRALEE

Words & Music by E.M. Spencer & C.W. Glover

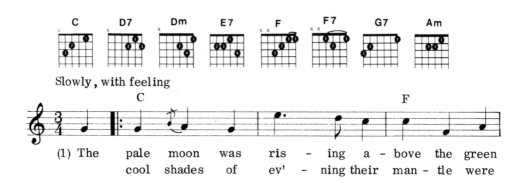

Slowly, with feeling

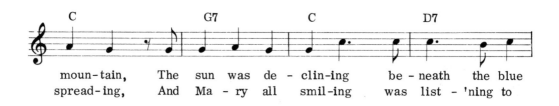

(1) The pale moon was ris - ing a - bove the green
cool shades of ev' - ning their man - tle were

moun-tain, The sun was de - clin-ing be - neath the blue
spread-ing, And Ma - ry all smil-ing was list - 'ning to

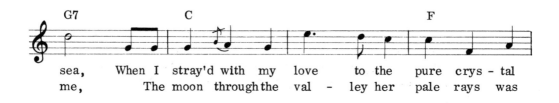

sea, When I stray'd with my love to the pure crys - tal
me, The moon through the val - ley her pale rays was

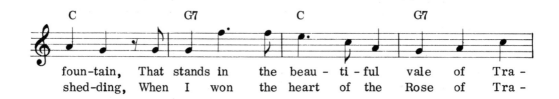

foun-tain, That stands in the beau - ti - ful vale of Tra -
shed-ding, When I won the heart of the Rose of Tra -

-lee. She was love-ly and fair as the rose of __ the __
-lee: Though__ love-ly and fair as the rose of __ the __

sum - mer, } Yet 'twas not her beau-ty a - lone that won
sum - mer, }

me, Oh, no! 'twas the truth in her eye ev - er

dawn - ing, That made me love Ma - ry, the Rose of Tra-

1
- lee.

2
(2) The

BEGORRAH

Words by Paddy Roberts
Music by Ray Martin

Be - gor-rah, me heart is all of a dith - er when
Skip-pin' a - long as light as a fea - ther and

ev - er she pass - es by, Be - gor-rah, there's al - ways
lead - in' the boys a dance, And all of the while I'm

some-bod-y with her but let 'em all go to the div - il, says I.
won - der-in' wheth-er I'm goin' to be giv - en the ghost of a chance.

Night or day I would-n't be let - tin' her far a - way from

out of me sight, All the oth - er fel-lows are get - tin' as

mad as a hat - ter, But what does it mat - ter. Be- gor-rah, at last, I've

off to paint the town to - night, Turn it up - side

down to - night, Oh Boy! What a par - ty.

Heigh Ho! Get ev - 'ry - one a -

round to - night. Beat the drum, and

get all the peo - ple to come. Be - gor-rah, at last, I've

man-aged to get her, the sun has be - gun to shine, She's

made up her mind, there's no - bod - y bet - ter, Be - gor-rah, to - mor - row she's

goin' to be mine.

THE HARP THAT ONCE

Traditional

(1) The harp that once through Ta - ra's halls it's soul of mus - ic shed, Now hangs as mute on Ta - ra's walls as if that soul were fled. So sleeps the pride of form - er days, so glo - ry's thrill is o'er; And hearts that once beat high for praise now feel that pulse no more.

(2) No more to chiefs and la - dies bright the harp of Ta - ra swells; The chord a - lone that breaks the night, it's tale of ru - in tells; Thus free - dom now so sel - dom wakes, the on - ly throb she gives, Is when some heart in-dig - nant breaks to show that still she lives.

D.C. Fine

MICK MCGILLIGAN'S BALL

Words & Music Michael Casey

(1) Mich - ael Ma - Gill - i - gan one fine day,
(2) All of the neigh-bours came from near and far,
(3) Flut - ers and fid - dle - rs danced a - round,

Got a lot of mon-ey from the U. S. A.
Mul - li - gan ar - rived there in a mo - tor car.
Drum-ming on the mole-skin made a love - ly sound.

All through the death of his Unc - le Joe,
Old Miss - us O' - Reil - ly bless her heart,
They blew a gale on the old trom - bone,

He got a mil - lion and a half or so, Says Ma-
Came with the fam - ily in a don - key cart. Pat O'-
Then reeled and roll-icked to the pip - er's drone. When they'd

-Gill - i - gan "I'll give a fan - cy ball,
-Raf - fer - ty ar - rived in an air - o - plane,
fin-ished with the whis - ky, beer and wine,

Down at the old an-cest-ral hall." In - vit - ed the neigh-bours
You'll nev-er see the like a - gain. And there was a shout when
They took a hand in "Auld Lang Syne," There ne'r was the like I

ev - 'ry - one, For to have some mu-sic and some rare old fun.
two old Skins, Came a-long at a gal-lop with two Miss Quinns.
do de -clare, Ask that grand old Hool-ey down in sweet Kil - dare.

CHORUS

mf And they all went down to

Mick Mc- Gill - i -gan's Ba - - - ll, Where they

had to tear the pa - per off the wa - - -

-ll, To make room for all the peo - ple in the

ha - - - ll, Oh, the girls and the boys made a

dev-il of a noise, At Mick Mc - Gill - i - gan's Ball.

Ball. B. A. dou-ble L Ball.

THE IRISH ROVER

Traditional

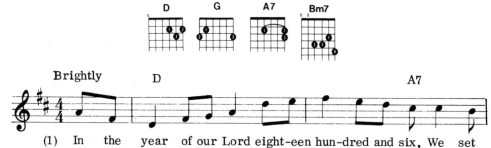

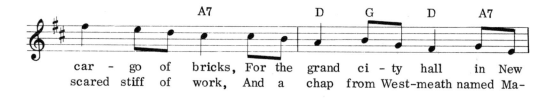

(1) In the year of our Lord eight-een hun-dred and six, We set
(2) There was Bar-ney Ma-gee from the banks of the Lee; There was

sail from the coal quay of Cork. We were sail-ing a-way with a
Ho-gan from Coun-ty Ty-rone. There was John-ny Mc-Gurk who was

car-go of bricks, For the grand ci-ty hall in New
scared stiff of work, And a chap from West-meath named Ma-

York. We'd an el-e-gant craft, it was rigged fore and aft, And
-lone. There was Slug-ger O'-Toole, who was drunk as a rule, And

how the trade winds drove _____ her; She had
fight-ing Bill Tra-cy from Do - ver; And your

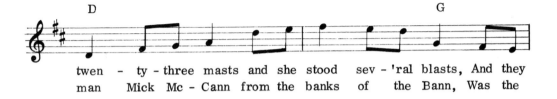

twen - ty - three masts and she stood sev - 'ral blasts, And they
man Mick Mc - Cann from the banks of the Bann, Was the

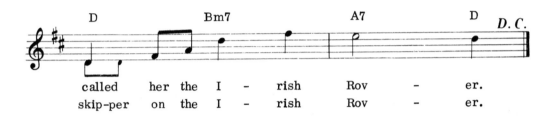

called her the I - rish Rov - er.
skip-per on the I - rish Rov - er.

(3) We had one million bags of the best Sligo rags,
    We had two million barrels of bone;
    We had three million bales of old nanny goat's tails,
    We had four million barrels of stone.
    We had five million hogs and six million dogs,
    And seven million barrels of porter;
    We had eight million sides of old blind horses' hides
    In the hold of the Irish Rover.

(4) We had sailed seven years when the measels broke out,
    And our ship lost her way in a fog.
    And the whole of the crew was reduced down to two;
    'Twas myself and the captain's old dog.
    Then the ship struck a rock, O Lord, what a shock,
    And nearly tumbled over;
    Turned nine times around, then the poor old dog was drowned.
    I'm the last of the Irish Rover.

COME BACK TO ERIN

Traditional

hush of the star - shine, O - ver the moun - tain, the

CHORUS

buffs and the bays! Then come back to E - rin, Ma-

-vour - neen, Ma - vour - neen, Come back a - gain to the

land of thy birth. _____ Come back to E - rin, Ma-

-vour-neen, Ma-vour-neen, And _ it's Kil-lar - ney shall ring with our mirth.

2. Over the green sea, Mavourneen, Mavourneen,
   Long shone the white sail that bore thee away.
   Riding the white waves that fair summer mornin',
   Just like a Mayflow'r afloat on the bay.
   O! but my heart sank when clouds came between us,
   Like a grey curtain the rain falling down,
   Hid from my sad eyes the path o'er the ocean,
   Far, far away where my colleen had flown.
   CHORUS

3. O! may the Angels awakin' and sleepin',
   Watch o'er my bird in the land far away.
   And it's my pray'rs will consign to their keepin',
   Care o' my jewel by night and by day.
   When by the fireside I watch the bright embers,
   Then all my heart flies to England and thee,
   Cravin' to know if my darlin' remembers,
   Or if her thoughts may be crossin' to me.
   CHORUS

THE WILD COLONIAL BOY

Traditional

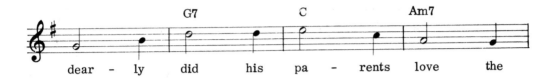

dear - ly did his pa - rents love the

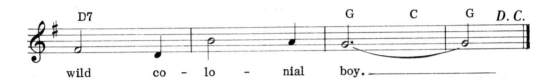

wild co - lo - nial boy.

(2) At the early age of sixteen years he left his native home,
And through Australia's sunny clime he was inclined to roam.
He robbed the lordly squatters, their flocks he would destroy,
A terror to Australia was the wild colonial boy.

(3) For two long years this daring youth ran on his wild career,
With a heart that knew no danger, their justice did not fear.
He stuck the Beechworth coach up and he robbed Judge McEvoy
Who, trembling, gave his gold up to the wild colonial boy.

(4) He bade the judge "Good morning" and he told him to beware,
For he never robbed an honest judge what acted "on the square",
"Yet you would rob a mother of her son and only joy,
And bred a race of outlaws like the wild colonial boy!"

(5) One morning on the prairie wild, Jack Duggan rode along,
While listening to the mocking birds singing a cheerful song,
Out jumped three troopers fierce and grim, Kelly, Davis and Fitzroy,
They all set out to capture him, the wild colonial boy.

(6) 'Surrender now Jack Duggan, you can see there's three to one,
Surrender in the Queen's name sir, you are a plundering son'.
Jack drew two pistols from his side and glared upon Fitzroy,
'I'll fight, but no surrender,' cried the wild colonial boy.

(7) He fired point blank at Kelly and brought him to the ground,
He fired a shot at Davis too, who fell dead at the sound.
But a bullet pierced his brave young heart from the pistol of Fitzroy,
And that was how they captured him, the wild colonial boy.

THE DEAR LITTLE SHAMROCK

Traditional

Moderato

G

mp

There's a dear lit - tle plant that

C **G** **D7** **G**

grows in our Isle, 'Twas Saint Pat - rick him -

E7 **A7** **D7**

-self sure that set it; _____ And the

G **C** **B7**

sun on his la - bour with plea - sure did

Em **G**

smile, And the dew from his eye oft - en

D7 **G** **C** **G** **D7**

wet it. _____ It shines thro' the

D7

bog, thro' the brake, thro' the mire - land, And he

called it the dear lit-tle Sham-rock of

CHORUS

Ire-land. The dear lit-tle Sham-rock, the

sweet lit-tle Sham-rock, the dear lit-tle,

sweet lit-tle Sham-rock of Ire-land.

2. That dear little plant still grows in our land,
   Fresh and fair as the daughters of Erin,
   Whose smiles can bewitch, and whose eyes can command,
   In each climate they ever appear in.
   For they shine thro' the bog, thro' the brake, thro' the mireland,
   Just like their own dear little Shamrock of Ireland.
   CHORUS

3. That dear little plant that springs from our soil,
   When its three little leaves are extended,
   Denotes from the stalk we together should toil,
   And ourselves by ourselves be befriended.
   And still thro' the bog, thro' the brake, thro' the mireland,
   From one root should branch, like the Shamrock of Ireland.
   CHORUS

THE MARCH HARE

Words & Music by Philip Green

di - dum dum.   Doo - dle oo - dle oo - dle oo -dle id-dle-ee

doo - dle oo - dle   oo - dle oo-dle id-dle-ee doo - dle oo - dle

oo - dle ee - dle i - doh - de doo-dle id-dle-ee oo - dle id-dle - ee

i   dum   dum.   i   dum   dum. Doo - dle-ee

di   di   di   doo - dle oo-dle-ee oo - dle oo -dle oo-dle-ee

doo-dle oo - dle oo - dle oo - dle oo - dle i - dle oo - dle oo-dle-ee

di   di   di   doo - dle oo-dle-ee oo - dle oo-dle oo-dle -ee

doo - dle oo - dle -ee doo - dle oo - dle-ee di dum dum.

71

LIMERICK IS BEAUTIFUL

Traditional

(1) Oh, ___ Li - mer-ick ___ is beau- ti -ful, as ev' - ry-bo - dy knows, ___ And by that Ci - ty of my heart, how proud old Shan - non flows. ___ It sweeps down by ___ the brave old town, ___ as pure in depth ___ and tone, As when Sars-field swept ___ the Sa-xons from the walls of Gar-ry - owen.

(2) 'Tis not for Limerick that I sigh though I love her in my soul,
Though times will change and friends will die and man will not control.
No, not for friends long passed away, or days forever flown,
But the maiden I adore, is sad in Garryowen.

(3) Oh, she I love is beautiful, and world-wide is her fame;
She dwells down by the rushing tide, and Eire is her name;
And dearer than my very life her glances are to me,
The light that guides my weary soul, across life's stormy sea.

(4) I loved her in my boyhood and now in manhood's noon,
The vision of my life is still to dry thy tears, aroon,
I'd sing unto the tomb or dance beneath the gallows tree,
To see her on the hills once more, proud, passionate and free.

PHIL THE FLUTER'S BALL

Traditional

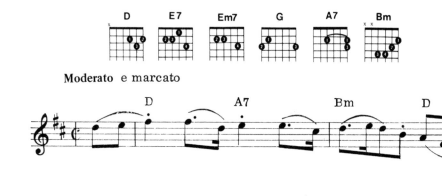

Moderato e marcato

(1) Have you

heard of Phil the Flu-ter, of the town of Bal - ly-muck? The —
(2) Mis-ther Den- is Dog-her-ty, who kep' "The Run-nin' Dog;" There was
(3) lit - tle Mick- y Mul -li-gan got up to show them how, And —
(4) Phil the Flu-ter tipped a wink to lit - tle crook-ed Pat, "I —

times were go - ing hard for him, in fact the man was bruk, So he
lit - tle crook-ed Pad -dy from the Tir - a-lough-ett bog: There were
then the wid -da' Caf-fer -ty steps out and makes her bow. "I could
think it's near - ly time", says he, "for pass - in' round the hat." So —

D   G   D

just sent out a no - tice to his neigh-bours, one and all, As
boys from ev-'ry Bar - on -y, and girls from ev -'ry "art," And the
dance you off your legs," says she, "as sure as you are born, If you
Pad- dy passed the cau-been round, and look - ing might-y cute, Sez, "Ye've

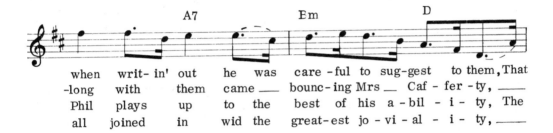
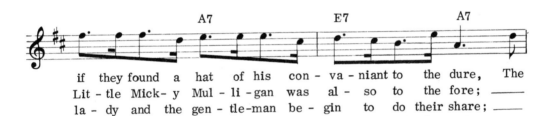

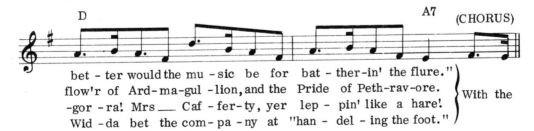

toot   of   the flute,   And   the   twid - dle   of   the   fid - dle, O'

Hop-ping in   the mid- dle, like   a   her-rin' on a grid-dle. O'____

Up,   down,   hands a - rown', Cross-in' to   the   wall,   Oh! ____

had - n't we   the gai - e - ty   at Phil   the Flu-ter's Ball! ____

1.2.3.

(2) There was
(3) First ____
(4) Then ____

MY WILD IRISH ROSE

Traditional

GALWAY BAY

Words & Music by Dr Arthur Colahan

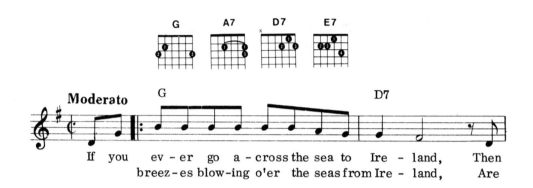

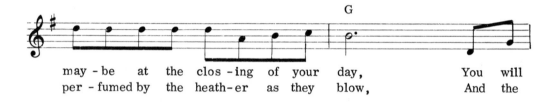

If you ev – er go a – cross the sea to Ire – land, Then
breez – es blow – ing o'er the seas from Ire – land, Are

may – be at the clos – ing of your day, You will
per – fumed by the heath – er as they blow, And the

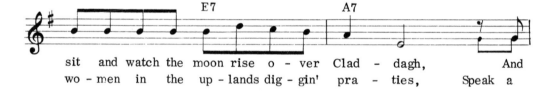

sit and watch the moon rise o – ver Clad – dagh, And
wo – men in the up – lands dig – gin' pra – ties, Speak a

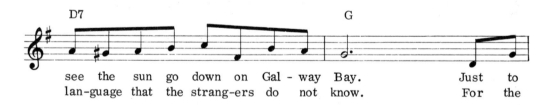

see the sun go down on Gal – way Bay. Just to
lan-guage that the strang-ers do not know. For the

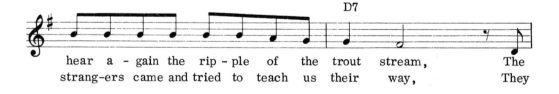

hear a – gain the rip – ple of the trout stream, The
strang-ers came and tried to teach us their way, They

wo-men in the mea-dows mak-ing hay, And to
scorn'd us just for be-ing what we are, But they

sit be-side a turf fire in the cab-in, And
might as well go chas-ing af-ter moon-beams, Or

watch the bare-foot Gos-soons at their play. For the
light a pen-ny can-dle from a

star. And if there is going to be a life here-

-aft-er, And some-how I am sure there's going to

be, I will ask my God to let me make my

hea-ven, In that dear land a-cross the I-rish sea.

THE MINSTREL BOY

Traditional

12/87